AND GOD CREATED

SCIENCE

EXPLORING OUTER SPACE

30 AMAZING PROJECTS THAT EXPLORE THE WONDERS OF GOD'S CREATION

STEPHANIE FINKE

PROMISE PRESS

An Imprint of Barbour Publishing

© 2000 by Stephanie Finke

ISBN 1-57748-884-9

Illustrations: Simon Shaw
Photography: © 1999 PhotoDisc., Inc.

Published by Promise Press, an imprint of Barbour Publishing, Inc., P.O. Box 719, Uhrichsville, Ohio 44683
www.barbourbooks.com

 Member of the
Evangelical Christian
Publishers Association

Printed in the United States of America.

TABLE OF CONTENTS

AND GOD CREATED SPACE

In the beginning God
created the heavens and the earth.
Now the earth was formless
and empty,
darkness was over
the surface of the deep,
and the Spirit of God
was hovering over the waters.
And God said, "Let there be light,"
and there was light.
God saw that the light was good,
and he separated the light from the darkness.
God called the light "day," and the darkness he called "night."
And there was evening, and there was morning—the first day.

Genesis 1:1–5

What a miracle! The earth, the universe, and everything in it was created by God. The story of creation was recorded by Moses, over 3,000 years ago, long before there were astronauts, telescopes, or any modern-day science. But due to God's divine inspiration, Moses understood that before God created the earth, the world was "formless and empty."

Current scientific theory fully supports what Moses wrote in 1440 B.C. Scientists believe that before the universe was created there was nothing, that all matter and time were created with the beginning of the universe. As Christians we understand that God is the Creator of all time and matter.

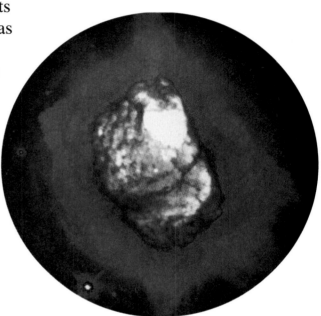

We can use the information gathered by scientists and researchers to give us a better understanding of how God's universe works.

Dear God,

Thank You for the miracle of Your creation. We praise You for the beauty of Your heavens and ask that You help us to use the knowledge of science to help us understand Your amazing universe.

In Christ's name we pray,

Amen.

DAY AND NIGHT

God called the light "day,"
and the darkness he called "night."
And there was evening,
and there was morning—the first day.
Genesis 1:5

When God created the world and set it spinning on its axis, He created day and night. To understand this you must realize that in basic terms, the earth is a giant sphere (like a ball), rotating on its axis, an invisible, slanted pole in space. The earth is in constant motion, making one complete turn every 24 hours. As the earth spins, the light from the sun reaches only a part of the world. The part of the earth facing the sun has daylight. The part of the earth that is turned away from the sun is dark and has night. You can see how the darkness is created by the earth's own shadow with this experiment.

To simulate night and day, use the inflated balloon to represent the earth.

You may want to draw the shapes of the continents, or you can simply make an X to mark the place where you live.

Darken the room and have one person hold the flashlight. Select another person to hold the balloon and spin it slowly between his two fingers. This spinning simulates the earth rotating on its axis.

Shine the flashlight on the balloon as it turns, and observe that as the X faces the light, there is daylight. As the X moves away from the flashlight, it is in the shadow of the balloon. This creates darkness, just as the shadow of the earth creates night.

What You Need:
- Flashlight
- Dark room
- Round, inflated balloon
- Permanent ink marker
- Two helpers

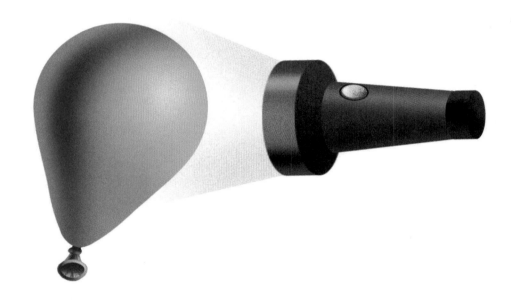

ME AND MY SHADOW

Keep me as the apple of your eye;
hide me in the shadow of your wings.
Psalm 17:8

It's hard to imagine, but Jesus and His disciples did not have clocks or wristwatches. They looked at the position of the sun and the shadows on the ground to tell time. You can learn to tell time with shadows, too.

Take a piece of butcher paper outside early in the morning. Tape it to the ground so it will not move. Have one person stand in the middle of the paper and draw an outline of his feet. This will mark the exact spot to stand each time.

Look at the paper and observe the shadow of the person standing on the paper. Outline the shadow with the marker and write the exact time on the outline. Return to the same spot every hour and outline the new shadow each time. Remember to record the time on each outline.

You will notice that shadows are longest in the morning and evening. They are shortest at noon when the sun is overhead. The shadows will also be in the opposite direction from which the sun is shining.

By observing the moving shadows and how they look at different times of the day, you can begin to tell time without a clock.

What You Need:

- Large piece of white butcher paper, 6 to 8 feet long
- Permanent ink marker
- Masking tape
- Open area of smooth ground or concrete
- A friend or helper

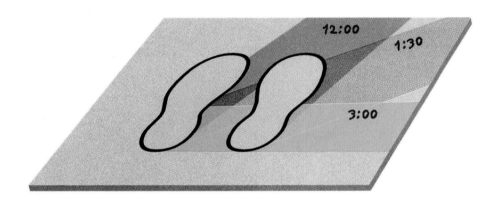

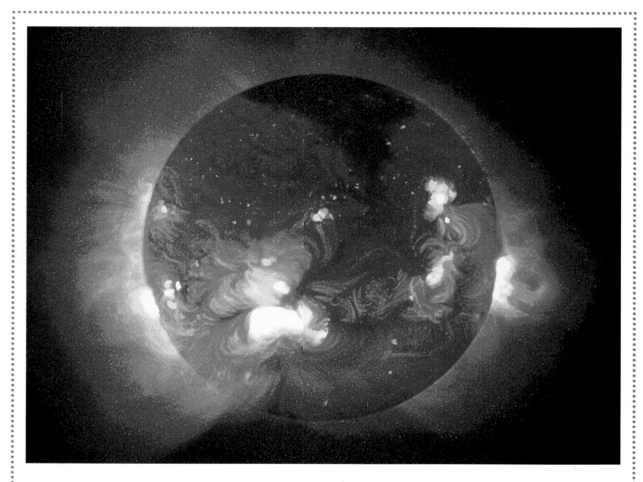

SUN TIME

Who made the great lights—
the sun to govern the day, . . .
the moon and stars to govern the night. . .
Psalm 136:7-9

During biblical times some people employed a type of clock called a sundial. This instrument used the moving shadows to help people tell time. Of course on cloudy days they had to rely on their stomachs to tell them when it was lunchtime. You can make your own sundial.

Lay a piece of cardboard on a flat surface outside in the sun. Have your adult helper use the knife to cut a hole in the center of the cardboard the diameter of the dowel rod. (Diameter is the measurement through the center of an object.) Insert the dowel rod into the hole perpendicular (straight up and down) to the cardboard. The dowel rod will cast a shadow on the cardboard. Use the marker to trace the line of the dowel rod's shadow. Write the time at the end of the line. Repeat this step on every hour. By sunset you will have a complete sundial. Observe the sundial during the next few days and see how accurately the shadows predict the time.

Wait a few weeks and take the sundial outside again. See if there are any changes to the way the shadows predict the time. Remember the earth is constantly moving in its orbit around the sun. How will this affect the sundial?

What You Need:
- Adult helper
- One thick piece of corrugated cardboard (at least 2 feet by 2 feet in size)
- One dowel rod
- Pointed knife
- Permanent ink marker
- Sunny day

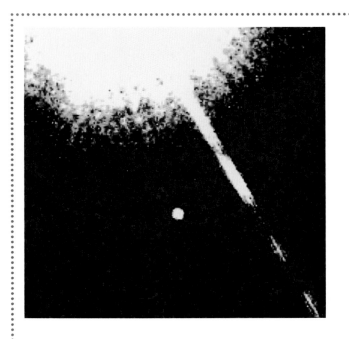

STAR LIGHT, SUN BRIGHT

*God made two great lights—
the greater light to govern the day
and the lesser light to govern the night.
He also made the stars.*

Genesis 1:16

Shining in the night, above the earth, are the stars and planets God created to fill His sky. The star closest to the earth is the sun. It is not larger than the other stars but since it is closer, it seems to be much brighter. The light of the sun shines so brightly in the sky that during the day its light blocks the glow of all other stars. Only when the earth is turned away from the sun and blocking the sun's rays, can human eyes see the stars.

You can demonstrate how the sun overpowers the light of more distant stars through a simple experiment.

Use a pencil to poke small holes in the bottom of the shoebox. Place the shoebox 3 feet from the wall and make sure the holes face the wall. Darken the room and shine a flashlight through the holes. You should see "stars" appear on the wall.

Now take the other flashlight, hold it 1 foot away from the wall and turn it on. What happens to the light from the "stars" in the shoebox? The flashlight nearer the wall appears brighter and blocks the light from the more distant "stars" just as the sun blocks the light of the stars during the day.

PLANETARY PROPORTIONS

Give thanks to the Lord of lords: . . .
to him who alone does great wonders, . . .
who by his understanding made the heavens. . . .
Psalm 136:3-5

Stars are not the only objects God created to fill the heavens. He also made planets like the ones in our solar system. Planets are large objects that orbit around a star or the sun. Our solar system contains nine planets. Three of the planets, Mercury, Venus, and Mars, are hard and rocky like Earth while the four largest planets, Jupiter, Saturn, Uranus, and Neptune, are made of gases and water. The smallest planet, Pluto, is a frozen ball of water and methane ice.

To get a better idea of the proportion and positions of the planets in our solar system, you can examine some familiar fruits.

Each of the pieces of fruit represents the size of one of the nine planets. Pick up the fruit and compare the sizes. How many Earths could you fit into one Jupiter? How many Plutos could fit into one Earth?

Line the fruit up in the order of their distance from the sun. Mercury is the closest planet followed by Venus, Earth, Mars, Jupiter, Saturn, Uranus, Neptune, and Pluto. Which planets do you think have the highest temperatures? Which planets are the coldest?

You will notice the sun is not a part of this model. The sun is so large that to include it in this scale, you would need a 10-foot watermelon!

After you are through examining your fruit planets, cut them into chunks and mix them in a bowl for a great solar system snack. As you eat your snack, remember that the God who created the planets also created the fruit.

What You Need:
- coconut / Jupiter
- grapefruit / Saturn
- oranges / Uranus and Neptune
- small strawberries / Venus, Earth, and Mars
- raisins / Mercury and Pluto

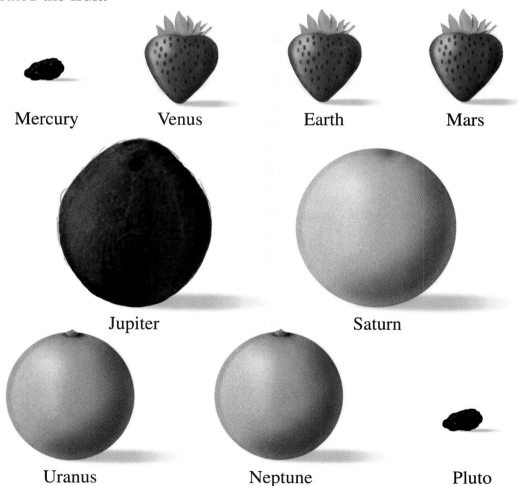

Mercury   Venus   Earth   Mars

Jupiter   Saturn

Uranus   Neptune   Pluto

GOD'S POWERFUL SUN

And God said, "Let there be light," and there was light.

Genesis 1:3

God's creation of the sun not only provided the world with light; it also gave heat and energy to the earth. Most of the energy people use is derived from the sun. Gas for cars, coal for heat, and oil for electrical energy all come from "fossil fuel," which is sunlight energy stored in ancient plants. Even wood that burns in the fireplace comes from the sunlight energy the tree stored as it grew in the forest.

Besides fossil fuels, the sun's energy can be used directly by solar power stations. Large solar mirrors collect the energy and make water boil. The steam from the water drives engines that in turn create electrical energy.

You can see the effect of the sun's energy in a simple chocolate chip experiment.

This experiment should be done inside where the temperature is constant. Place the chocolate chips in the bowl. Make sure the chocolate chips are solid before you begin the experiment.

Place the bowl of chocolate chips in front of a sunny window and use a magnifying glass to capture the sunlight and direct the rays onto a single chocolate chip for a few moments. What happens? How are the other chips in the bowl affected?

What other ways could you use the energy of God's sun?

What You Need:
- 1 handful of real chocolate chips
- Magnifying glass
- Bowl
- Bright sunny day
- Adult supervision

'ROUND THEY GO

*The sun stopped in the middle of the sky
and delayed going down about a full day.
There has never been a day like it before or since,
a day when the LORD listened to a man.
Surely the LORD was fighting for Israel!*

Joshua 10:13–14

The story of God stopping the sun for a day is even more miraculous when you understand the way the universe works.

God created the universe to be in constant motion. The planets spin on their axes, the moons circle their planets, planets revolve around stars, and even the stars themselves spin. Scientists believe that entire galaxies actually rotate.

By stopping the earth from revolving around the sun, God temporarily stopped His own laws of gravity. Amazingly, the earth did not float into the sun, get hit by another planet, or suffer any serious consequences.

To gain a better understanding of how miraculous this was, try this simple experiment:

Use the nail to punch two holes in the cup. Place the holes exactly opposite of each other. Thread one end of the

What You Need:

- 4 feet of string
- Plastic or paper cup
- Nail
- 1/4 cup water
- Clear, open area outdoors

string through one hole and tie it at the end. Then take the other end of the string and thread it through the opposite hole and tie that end. It should look like you have created a very long handle for your cup. (See Image A.)

Pour the water into your cup. Grab the end of the string and stand in a clear area outdoors where you will not hit anything. Quickly swing the cup in a circular motion toward the sky. Keep spinning the cup. Amazingly the water will not spill. (See Image B.)

This is centrifugal force at work, and it is one of the reasons the planets stay in orbit around the sun. Centrifugal force is the outward force felt when moving in a circle. Centrifugal force is really the tendency of a body to move in a straight line rather than a circle but combined with the pull of gravity, it keeps the planets in orbit around the sun.

The water is like the planet Earth staying in orbit around the sun. What happens if you suddenly stop spinning your cup of water? Imagine what would happen if the earth suddenly stopped moving. What a miracle God made for Joshua and Israel when He stopped the earth for a day.

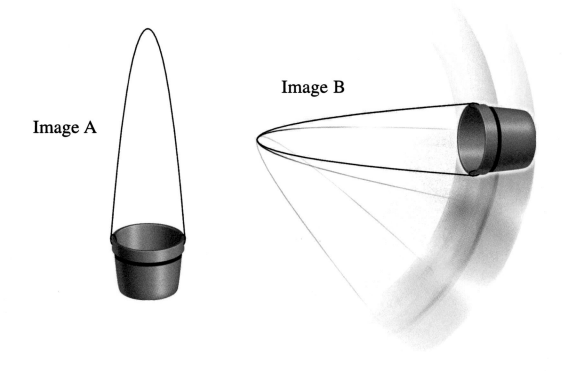

Image A

Image B

GOD MADE NINE

By the word of the LORD were the heavens made,
their starry host by the breath of his mouth.

Psalm 33:6

When God created our solar system, He placed nine planets in orbit around the sun. But it has taken scientists centuries to locate and name all the planets. As a matter of fact, humans have only known about the existence of Pluto since 1930.

The first six planets from the sun—Mercury, Venus, Earth, Mars, Jupiter, and Saturn—were discovered and named by ancient astronomers. These planets were close enough to Earth that they could be seen in the night sky with the naked eye. Uranus was the first planet discovered after the invention of the telescope and was officially declared a planet in 1781.

Early in the ninth century, scientists used mathematical equations to predict the probability of two planets beyond Uranus, but Neptune was not "seen" by an astronomer until 1846. Nearly a century later, Pluto was discovered and named as the ninth and smallest planet in the solar system.

Today researchers use very powerful telescopes and observatories to study the skies. With the aid of the Hubble telescope orbiting Earth, scientists have learned a great deal about the size and surface of each of the nine planets in God's solar system.

The telescope has been a necessary tool for space research. Even the planets closest to Earth are millions of miles away. You can take a "space walk" to get a better understanding of the distances in space.

Before you go outside, use the paper and markers to create a sign for each planet and one for the sun. Tape each sign to one craft stick (or twig) allowing enough room at the bottom of the stick so that the stick may be placed in the ground.

You will be making a model of the distance between the planets in the solar system. For this model the scale will be:

1 inch = 1 million miles

Use the chart at the bottom of this page as a guide. You can use a tape measure to accurately place each sign or you can do an approximate walk, keeping in mind that one adult stride or step is about 3 feet long, and an average adult male's foot is about 12 inches long.

Once outside, place the sun sign in the ground. This represents the sun's place in the solar system. Walk 36 inches (3 feet) away from the sun and place the Mercury sign in the ground. Continue walking in a straight line from Mercury for 31 more inches and place the sign for Venus in the

What You Need:

- This is an outdoor activity and requires a large, open space
- Paper
- Permanent ink markers
- Tape
- 10 jumbo craft sticks or 10 strong twigs
- Tape measure

DISTANCE CHART

1 inch = 1 million miles

Mercury	36 inches	Saturn	403 inches
Venus	31 inches	Uranus	896 inches
Earth	26 inches	Neptune	1,011 inches
Mars	48 inches	Pluto	872 inches
Jupiter	342 inches		

ground. Place the Earth sign 26 inches from Venus and the Mars sign 48 inches from Earth (about 11 ¾ feet from the sun). These are the inner planets, called that because they are the closest to the sun.

To begin placing the signs for the outer planets, you will need to walk 342 inches (28 ½ feet) from Mars and put the Jupiter sign in the ground. Notice how much space is between Mars and Jupiter. Part of that space contains the asteroid belt. The Saturn sign can be placed 403 inches (about 33 ½ feet) from Jupiter. Uranus should be 896 inches (about 74 ¾ feet) from Saturn. Stand by the Uranus sign and look back at the Earth sign. Do you understand why it took the invention of the telescope for scientists to find the last three planets?

You will need to walk 1,011 inches (about 84 ¼ feet) from Uranus to put the Neptune sign in the ground and 872 inches (about 72 ½ feet) from Neptune for Pluto. As you stand at the end of your "solar system" take a moment to look back to the sun (more than 300 feet away). Remember that each inch of ground you walked equals one million miles in space.

The size of God's creation is so immense, it is difficult for the human mind to comprehend.

SWING TIME

For a thousand years in your sight are like a day that has just gone by, or like a watch in the night.

Psalm 90:4

What You Need:
- Eight assistants
- Yarn in nine different colors
- Scissors
- Dowel rod or broomstick (handle only)
- Open space outside
- Masking tape
- Pen
- Distance Chart (on page 26)

Each planet in the solar system orbits the sun. For Earth, this trip around our star takes 365 ¼ days. We call this revolution a year. Planets that are closer to the sun complete their orbit in less time than Earth. For example, Mercury spins around the sun in only 88 days and Venus makes its orbit in only 225 days, so a "year" on Mercury and Venus would be much shorter than on Earth.

Being farther from the sun makes a planet's orbit longer. Circling the sun takes Mars almost twice as long as Earth, making the Martian year 687 Earth days long. The planet farthest from the sun has the longest year. Tiny Pluto, circling on the edge of the solar system, takes 90,800 Earth days to orbit the sun, or 248 Earth years.

Planets do vary in the speed of their orbit, but distance from the sun is the greatest factor in determining the length of a year.

You can learn how distance affects the revolution time with a simple experiment.

Select a color of yarn to represent each of the planets. Measure out 1 centimeter of yarn per 1 million miles from the sun. For example: Mercury is 36 million miles from the sun so you should measure out 36 centimeters of yarn. Add 4 centimeters to the total amount to be cut. This allows extra yarn for tying. So Mercury would have 40 centimeters of yarn, Venus would have 71 centimeters of yarn, and Earth would have 97 centimeters of yarn, and so on.

After you have cut the correct amount of yarn for each planet, label each piece of yarn with the planet's name, using a piece of masking tape and a pen.

Place the dowel rod or the broomstick firmly in the ground. Tie one end of each string to the rod. Give the other end of each string to a person. Line all the people up in a row holding their planet's string. This represents the position of the planets in order of distance from the sun.

Now have the "planets" begin walking slowly around the pole (the sun) keeping their string taut (straight, not drooping). The people should all move at the same pace. (Because the "outer planets" travel farther, this works best if they hold their strings behind the "inner planets" when they line up.) Notice how quickly the person holding the Mercury string completes the revolution. The revolution represents one year for each planet.

The person holding the Pluto string will be the last to complete his revolution due to the length of the string, or in other words, the distance from the sun.

DISTANCE CHART
Miles from the Sun (millions)

Mercury	Venus	Earth	Mars	Jupiter	Saturn	Uranus	Neptune	Pluto
36	67.2	93	141.6	483.6	886.7	1,783	2,794	3,666

HOW LONG IS A DAY?

This is the day the LORD has made;
let us rejoice and be glad in it.
Psalm 118:24

Not every planet has the same length of day. God created the earth to spin, or rotate, on its axis once every 24 hours. This 24-hour period of light and dark is called one day and is a basic measurement of time on Earth, but not all planets spin at the same speed.

Mars has a rotation time closest to Earth's and spins on its axis once every 25 hours. On Mars you would see the sun set and rise in one 25-hour period. But visitors to Jupiter and Saturn would see the sun rise and set every 10 hours. These planets spin faster on their axes than Earth and Mars.

The planet with the slowest "spin" is Venus. It rotates on its axis only once every 5,832 hours or once every 243 Earth days. Mercury also has a very slow rotation. It spins on its axis only once every 59 Earth days. Mercury has 29 Earth days of night before the sun rises again.

The amount of sunlight on each side of a planet makes a huge difference in temperature. During the "night" of Mercury, temperatures can drop to

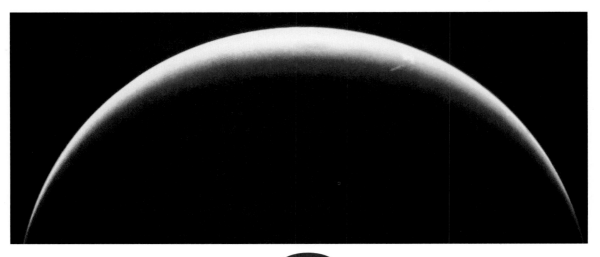

- Corrugated cardboard box
- Two thermometers
- Sunny window

-290 degrees Fahrenheit (-180 degrees Celsius), even though Mercury is the planet closest to the sun.

To better understand how sunlight affects temperature, try this experiment. Place the bottom of the cardboard box so that it is facing the window. This should block all sun from the interior of the box. This will represent a planet during the night. Place one thermometer inside the box.

Put the other thermometer next to the box, in the sun. This represents the planet during the daytime. Check the thermometers in 10 minutes and see if you can tell a difference.

You may want to try this experiment again outside and see if your results are the same.

The amount of light and heat a planet receives determine whether it can sustain life. God gave Earth the perfect combination of day and night.

SLANTED PLANETS

The heavens are yours,
and yours also the earth;
you founded the world and all that is in it.
You created the north and the south....
Psalm 89:11-12

Every planet has an axis. An axis is an imaginary line or pole around which a planet rotates. For Earth this pole runs from the north to the south. It is easy to visualize an axis by looking at a globe. When you spin the globe, it whirls around on the axis.

The earth turns on its axis from east to west. It spins at a slight tilt of 23 degrees.

Both Mars and Saturn have axis alignments similar to Earth with an axis tilt of 27 degrees. Mercury is the only planet in the solar system to spin on a perfectly straight axis. Its tilt is 0 degrees.

The most unusual planet rotation belongs to Uranus. It rolls along on its side with an axis tilted 97.9 degrees.

You can compare the tilt of the

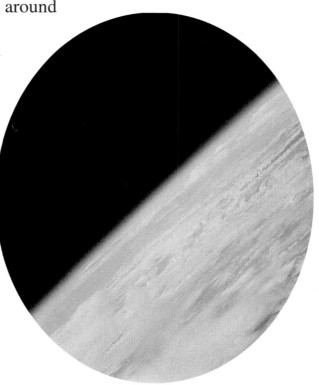

What You Need:
- planet tilt chart
- nine small dowel rods, 6 to 8 inches long (pencils may also be used)
- Toothpicks
- Modeling clay
- Paper and pen

planets' axes by building clay models. Make an enlarged copy of the planet tilt chart (see page 33).

This will be your guide for making the model planets. Make nine balls of clay to represent the nine planets. They do not have to be made to scale, but keep in mind that the planets from biggest to smallest: Jupiter, Saturn, Uranus, Neptune, Earth, Venus, Mars, Mercury, and Pluto.

After you have created the clay balls for the planets, use three toothpicks to create a tripod at the base of each planet so they will "stand" on a flat surface.

One by one, hold the clay "planets" next to the planet tilt chart. Line up the dowel with the line for the axis of that planet. Push the dowel through at the matching angle. Use the paper and pen to make labels that tell the name of each planet and its degree of tilt.

Now look at your model. Did God create a North Pole and South Pole for each planet? How do you think the tilt of each planet may affect the "weather" or seasons?

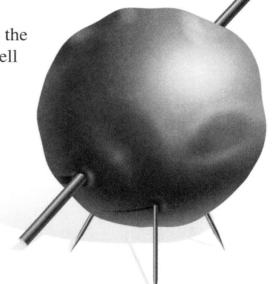

SEASONS SIMPLIFIED

And God said, "Let there be lights in the expanse of the sky to separate the day from the night, and let them serve as signs to mark seasons and days and years, and let them be lights in the expanse of the sky to give light on the earth." And it was so.

Genesis 1:14-15

God's design of the earth is quite amazing. Not only does the earth spin on its axis at 1,000 miles an hour; it also orbits around the sun at 6,500 miles per hour. This revolution takes place every 365 ¼ days.

Some parts of the world have seasons that change through the year, while other areas have temperatures that are almost always the same. This is caused by the tilt of the earth's axis and its sphere shape (round). Because the rays of the sun fall unevenly on a sphere, some parts of the earth receive more sunlight than other parts of the earth. This uneven light causes some areas of the world to receive more energy, or heat, than other areas.

The tilt of the earth's axis also causes the amount of daylight to change as the planet moves around the sun. The tilt of the axis remains constant during the entire revolution. This means people living in the hemisphere (half of the sphere) leaning toward the sun have longer days, or summer. When the same hemisphere is leaning away from the sun, the days are shorter and it is winter.

To see how the sun's rays fall on the earth, try this experiment:

Use the Styrofoam ball as a model of the earth. Look at a picture of the earth or a globe and use the permanent marker to trace an outline of the continents onto the ball. Use the picture below as a guide to insert the pencil through the Styrofoam ball.

The pencil represents Earth's axis. Now, darken the room and turn on the flashlight. Place the Styrofoam "globe" 3 to 4 feet from the light. Hold the pencil and spin it slowly to show the rotation of the earth. Notice that the light is brighter as it hits the middle of the ball and less intense at the top and bottom. This is what happens with the sun's rays.

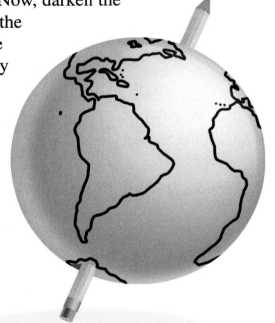

Follow the planet tilt chart and examine the way the light falls on your Styrofoam "globe" to see how the tilt of the earth's axis gives us the long, warm days of summer and short, cold days of winter.

PLANET TILT CHART

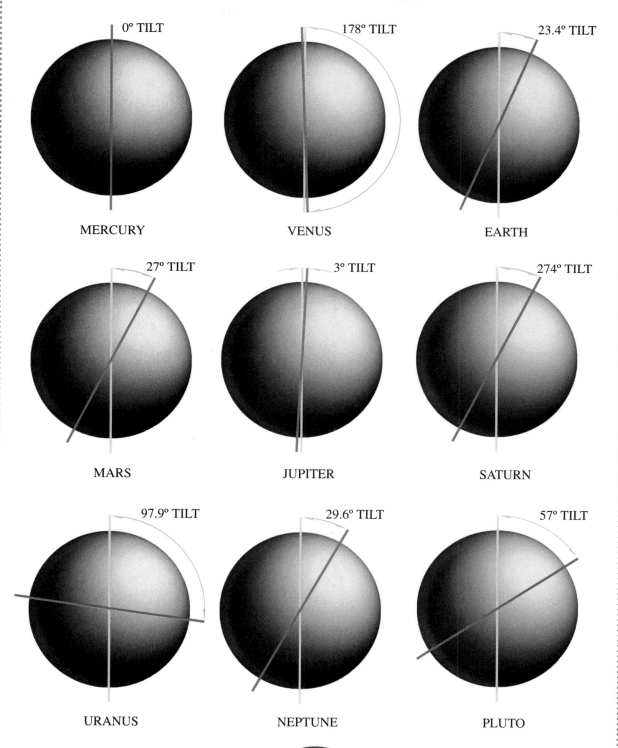

0° TILT

MERCURY

178° TILT

VENUS

23.4° TILT

EARTH

27° TILT

MARS

3° TILT

JUPITER

274° TILT

SATURN

97.9° TILT

URANUS

29.6° TILT

NEPTUNE

57° TILT

PLUTO

MERCURY'S MISHAPS

In the heavens he has pitched a tent for the sun,

It rises at one end of the heavens

and makes its circuit to the other;

nothing is hidden from its heat.

Psalm 19:4, 6

Orbiting closest to the sun is the solar system's second smallest planet, Mercury. Because it is so close to the sun, Mercury has extremely high daytime temperatures, sometimes reaching above 750 degrees Fahrenheit (400 degrees Celsius).

Amazingly, Mercury can also be extremely cold. Nighttime temperatures can drop to -290 degrees Fahrenheit (-180 degrees Celsius) because of Mercury's very slow rotation.

Mercury spins on its axis only once every 59 Earth days. The result of this slow spin is that one side of the planet remains in darkness away from the heat of the sun for nearly 28 Earth days.

Mercury is a rocky planet with no real atmosphere and a surface covered with craters. These craters were formed when comets and meteors slammed into Mercury. The shock of the impact usually causes the objects to explode and creates a deep hole in the ground. The crater made by a meteor is usually much larger than the meteor itself. Mercury has more craters than any other planet in the solar system.

What You Need:

- newspaper
- 4 to 5 cups of flour
- Marbles
- Metal baking pan

You can conduct an experiment to see how craters form on Mercury.

Spread the flour over the bottom of the baking pan. Make sure the flour is at least ½-inch deep. Add more flour if necessary. Cover the floor with the newspapers and place the baking pan in the center. The flour represents the surface of Mercury.

Stand over the baking pan holding the marbles. Carefully drop the marbles one at a time into the pan of flour. The marble represents a meteor that hit the planet's surface. Notice how much larger the print of the impact is compared to the marble.

The effect of a meteor hit would be the same on Earth or any other solid surfaced planet or moon. You may wonder why the earth is not covered in crater marks like Mercury. It is due to the thick atmosphere God placed around Earth. This atmosphere causes friction and burns up most meteors before they ever touch the ground. Friction is the force created by one object rubbing against another. You can feel the effect of friction by rubbing your hands together for 15 seconds.

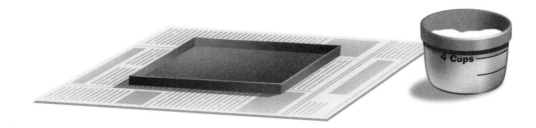

GREENHOUSE ON VENUS

...O morning star,
son of the dawn!
Isaiah 14:12

Since biblical days, people have been fascinated with the morning star. Next to the sun and moon, it is the brightest object in our sky but it is not a star at all. This bright, shining object is the planet Venus.

Venus has a thick cloud atmosphere that strongly reflects sunlight. This same thick atmosphere also helps trap the heat of the sun on the planet's surface making Venus the hottest planet in the solar system with a surface temperature of 900 degrees Fahrenheit (480 degrees Celsius). This thick atmosphere warms up the surface much like a greenhouse warms up plants. That is why it is called the greenhouse effect.

Venus's atmosphere is made up of carbon dioxide gas and clouds that contain droplets of sulfuric acid. These clouds are chased across the face of the planet by winds that can reach speeds of up to 220 miles per hour. These conditions make Venus a difficult planet to explore.

What You Need:

- Empty glass jar
- Plastic wrap
- Two thermometers
- Sunny window
- Modeling Clay
- Two pieces of 10-inch by 10-inch cardboard (same color)
- Permanent ink marker

Russian scientists were successful in sending a space probe through the atmosphere on Venus in 1967. But due to the harsh conditions, it only lasted 94 minutes before the thick atmosphere crushed it.

You can create and experiment to demonstrate how the atmosphere on Venus causes a greenhouse effect.

Label one piece of cardboard "atmosphere." Label the other piece of cardboard "no atmosphere." Place a small piece of clay on the "no atmosphere" cardboard and lay the thermometer in the clay.

Place the other thermometer inside the glass jar and put plastic wrap over the opening of the jar. The jar and the plastic wrap represent the atmosphere of Venus. The jar will act like the atmosphere by trapping the heat of the sun.

Use a few pieces of clay to secure the jar to the cardboard so it will not roll away. Lay the jar on the cardboard and place both pieces of cardboard by the same sunny window. Leave them for 10 to 15 minutes. When you return, check the difference in the temperatures of the thermometers.

GOD'S BLUE PLANET

The highest heavens belong to the LORD,
but the earth he has given to man.
Psalm 115:16

Venus is hot, Pluto is freezing, and Uranus spins on its side. Learning about the other planets in our solar system can make us grateful for the gift of life God gave to us on Earth.

When God created Earth, He gave the planet a protective atmosphere. This atmosphere is thick enough to trap the heat caused by the sun's rays but thin enough to let excess heat escape.

Earth is the only planet in the solar system to have liquid water on its surface. Constantly moving air creates wind. The wind in turn creates weather systems that provide rain to water the land and give fresh water to plants, animals, and people. Through His gift of atmosphere and water, God has made the miraculous, life-rich planet we call Earth.

- *Dark room*
- *Flashlight*
- *Measuring spoons*
- *Large glass jar*
- *Water*
- *Milk*

Viewed from outer space, Earth seems to have a blue halo around it. This is the atmosphere. Try this experiment to learn why the atmosphere looks blue.

Fill the glass jar with water and pour in 1 tablespoon of milk. Turn out the lights in the room and shine the flashlight through the glass jar. It should appear to be a blue-gray color.

The water in the jar represents the earth's atmosphere. The milk represents particles in the atmosphere. The particles in the earth's atmosphere are mainly dust and gas vapors. As they spread through the atmosphere, they reflect the white light and break it up into the colors of the rainbow. The particles absorb all the colors except the blue rays. These shine through and give the atmosphere its blue color.

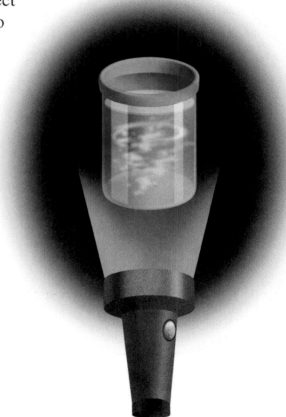

MARS MATTER

You alone are the LORD.
You made the heavens,
even the highest heavens,
and all their starry host,
the earth and all that is on it,
the seas and all that is in them.
You give life to everything,
and the multitudes of heaven worship you.
Nehemiah 9:6

In many ways Mars is very similar to Earth. It has a hard, rocky surface, a tilted axis that gives it seasons, and ice caps at both of its poles. Mars also has a rotation of just a little over 24 hours, giving it a day and night like Earth's. But there, the similarities end.

Mars is only ⅓ the size of Earth and has a weak gravitational pull. It is unable to hold a thick, protective atmosphere, so the surface temperature of Mars can fall to a chilly -190 degrees Fahrenheit (-123 degrees Celsius).

Because of the cold temperature, there is no liquid water on Mars. Instead, the surface of Mars is covered with a thick, red dust. The nearly constant Martian wind causes huge dust storms and gives the sky a pinkish color.

The red dust and soil on Mars tell scientists that at one time there may have been liquid water on Mars. The soil on Mars is red because of a process called oxidation. At one point in time, the iron in the Martian soil combined with water. When the liquid water evaporated out of the soil, the soil became rusty, or oxidized.

What You Need:
- Adult help
- Scissors
- Steel wool
- Glass or plastic pan
- 3 cups sand
- 1 cup potting soil
- Water
- Mixing bowl
- Wooden spoon

Try this experiment to demonstrate how the Martian soil got its color.

Mix the sand and the soil together in the bowl. Have your adult helper cut the steel wool into ½-inch pieces and add this to the soil and sand. Stir it all together. This is your "Martian soil."

Pour the mixture into the bottom of the pan. Pour enough water into the pan to cover the Martian soil.

Set the pan in a sunny window and check it once a day. The sun will evaporate the water so you will need to add moisture if it feels dry. Observe the soil for a week. How long does it take to make the soil turn red? Now you can understand how God created a "Red Planet."

STORMY JUPITER

When I consider your heavens,
the work of your fingers, the moon and the stars,
which you have set in place...
Psalm 8:3

The largest planet God put in the solar system is Jupiter. Unlike the four planets closest to the sun (Mercury, Venus, Earth, and Mars), Jupiter does not have a solid surface. It is a huge ball of swirling gas surrounding a small, rocky core. Jupiter has a diameter 11 times larger than Earth and contains 2.5 times the mass (the material that makes up the planet and gives it weight) of all the other planets combined.

For all its giant size and mass, Jupiter is a fast-moving planet. Jupiter spins on its axis once every 9 (Earth) hours. This causes Jupiter to have wind speeds up to 400 miles per hour. On Earth, winds of 100 miles per hour are considered hurricane force.

These fast winds cause violent storms to race across the surface of Jupiter. One famous storm is known as the Giant Red Spot. Astronomers first reported seeing it over 300 years ago. This storm is so big it could hold two Earths.

You can create a model of Jupiter's giant storm.

Mix the glue and water together in the bowl until it is milky. Place two drops of red food coloring and two drops of yellow food coloring on the mixture. This represents the atmosphere of Jupiter.

Use the straw to create wind on Jupiter's "atmosphere" by blowing gently on the surface of the glue and water mixture. You will see the red and yellow swirl together to form a storm "vortex" similar to a tornado or whirlwind.

What You Need:
- Measuring spoons
- Glass bowl
- 4 cups warm tap water
- 1 cup white school glue
- Straw
- Red and yellow liquid food coloring
- Spoon

THE FLOATING PLANET

*O LORD, our Lord, how majestic
is your name in all the earth!
You have set your glory above the heavens.
Psalm 8:1*

One of the most majestic sights in God's universe must be the planet Saturn. This gas giant is the second largest planet in our solar system. It has 18 moons and is surrounded by a colorful belt of rings made from orbiting chunks of ice and dust.

The rings of Saturn extend 260,000 miles out from the planet's surface. If the earth had rings this big, they would almost touch the moon.

Saturn is not only famous as a spectacular sight in God's heavens; it is

also amazingly lightweight. Saturn is about 94 percent hydrogen gas and 6 percent helium with small traces of ammonia, methane, and water vapors. These gases weigh less than water, so if there was an ocean

What You Need:

- *A bowl of water*
- *Marble*
- *Small, round balloon*

large enough, Saturn could actually float.

By comparison, Earth is dense and heavy. Made from rocks and metal, the earth would sink to the bottom of any ocean in the galaxy.

You can compare the densities of Earth and Saturn with a simple experiment.

Inflate the balloon until it is about 3 inches in diameter, then tie it off. The balloon is filled with air or gas and represents the density of Saturn. It has very little matter (or material) packed into a large space. Hold it in your hand and compare its weight to the marble. The marble is smaller but heavier. This means it has more matter packed into a smaller space. The marble represents the density of Earth.

Drop both the marble and the balloon into the water. Even though the balloon is larger, it floats because it is less dense than the marble. The same is true of Earth and Saturn. Saturn is less dense because it is mainly gas while Earth is made of rock and is much denser.

THE TWINS

*In the beginning you laid
the foundations of the earth,
and the heavens are the work of your hands.
Psalm 102:25*

Spinning around the sun at the far edge of the solar system are Uranus and Neptune. Similar in size and both made of gas, these planets were long considered to be twins. But when the Voyager 2 spacecraft took pictures of Neptune in 1989, scientists learned that the surfaces of the planets were quite different. It seems that in God's universe, even twins are unique.

Uranus is the most featureless planet in the solar system. It has very few clouds and no solid surface. Uranus is unique because it spins on its side with its axis being horizontal rather than vertical like the other planets.

Neptune's gas surface in not as calm as Uranus. The atmosphere of Neptune contains many large cloud formations. These clouds cause huge storm systems that can grow to be as large as the entire Earth.

Compare the "twin" planets by making a model of each planetary system. Roll the modeling clay into balls roughly the same size. Make one ball just slightly larger in diameter than the other ball. This is not a scale model and will simply

What You Need:

- Blue, green, and yellow modeling clay
- Two pieces of foam core board, 10 inches by 10 inches
- Pen
- Toothpicks
- Index cards

be used to show the similarities and differences of the planets.

Place the larger blue ball on a toothpick and put it in the center of one of the foam core boards. Use the index cards and pen to make a label for the planet Uranus.

Use a small amount of green modeling clay to make storms for Neptune and put them on the blue ball near the equator or middle. Place this ball on a toothpick in the center of the other foam core board and label this planet Neptune.

Next make 25 small yellow balls. These will represent the moons of each planet. Put them on toothpicks and place 17 of the moons around Uranus. Place the other 8 moons in orbit around Neptune. Let the modeling clay dry, and you will have a model of God's "twin" planets.

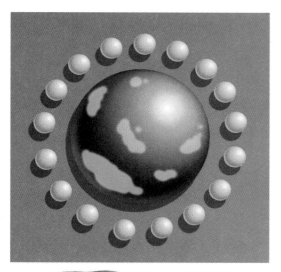

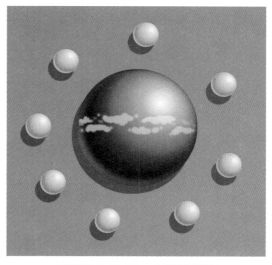

PLUTO'S PATH

Do you know the laws of the heavens?
Can you set up God's dominion over the earth?

Job 38:33

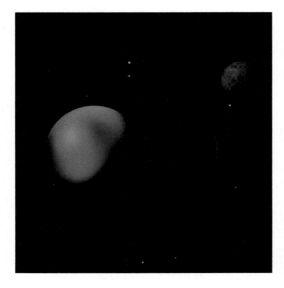

Pluto is the planet farthest from the sun. Or is it? God placed the planet Pluto in orbit around our sun along with the other planets, but until 1930, people thought that the solar system had only eight planets. It took an American scientist named Clyde Tombaugh to discover what God already knew; there was a ninth planet orbiting the sun.

Scientists have since discovered that Pluto has an orbit different than the other planets. Instead of a circular orbit, Pluto has an oval or tilted orbit. This means that for most of its 249-year orbit, Pluto is the planet farthest away from the sun. But during a 20-year period, it swings closer to the sun and Neptune becomes the last planet in the solar system. Or is it?

Scientists are still studying the gravitational pull of the planets and their orbits. In 1978 researchers discovered Pluto's moon, Charon. Because Charon is very large for a moon and orbits so close to Pluto, many astronomers think this pair may be a double planet system.

Some scientists think that there may even be a tenth planet in the solar system orbiting so far out from the sun that it has not yet been seen. Scientists call this unknown planet, Planet X.

They think that Planet X may have a very long and tilted orbit. Other astronomers believe that the measurements made of the gravitational pull on Uranus and Neptune are inaccurate and that Planet X does not exist. It may take many years of research for scientists to learn exactly how many planets God has placed in our solar system.

Try this simple demonstration to learn about the different orbital paths.

Stand in the middle of your open space and pull out 3 feet of rope. Let this rope dangle from your hand while you grasp the remainder of the rope. In this demonstration, your body represents the sun, and the rope represents the orbit of the planets. Stretch your arm out, and spin quickly so that your jump rope spins with you. (Make sure no one is close to you when you spin.) Your rope should be moving horizontally (circling you an even distance from the ground). This is the basic orbit of the nine known planets.

Now take the jump rope and swing it so it makes a circle perpendicular to the ground (straight up and down). This is the proposed orbit of Planet X. Since it may not be orbiting with the other planets, this may make it very difficult for scientists to find.

Planet X is just one more mystery in God's magnificent universe.

A COMET'S TALE

After Jesus was born in Bethlehem in Judea,
during the time of King Herod,
Magi from the east came to Jerusalem and asked,
"Where is the one who has been
born king of the Jews?
We saw his star in the east
and have come to worship him."
Matthew 2:1-2

Did God place a comet in the sky to announce the birth of His Son, Jesus?

Comets are some of the most spectacular sights in the night sky. With glowing tails that trail 50 million miles across the sky, comets are easily seen by the naked eye and would have made a spectacular welcome for the newborn King.

Scientists believe comets are made from the ice and dirt left over when God created the solar system. Masses of these chunks are in the outer reaches of the solar system in an area called the Kuiper Belt. Sometimes a piece of ice will leave the belt and will be pulled into orbit around the sun. As this chunk of ice moves toward the sun it starts to evaporate and produce trails of steam and gas. The sun reflects light off this gas, and we see this as the comet's tail.

Some comets appear in the sky and are only seen once. This is because comets evaporate from the sun's heat and wind. Some comets are large enough that they can remain in orbit around the sun for many years before they completely evaporate. One famous comet that is still orbiting in the solar system is Halley's Comet. Edmond Halley first discovered it in 1705. He predicted that the comet would pass by Earth again in 1758. He was correct, and the comet was named after him. The last time Halley's Comet was in the sight of Earth was in 1986, and it is predicted to pass by again in 2062.

It is the bright, glowing tail of the comet that makes it such a magnificent sight. The tail of the comet always streams away from the sun because it is blown back by the solar winds. This makes a comet that is moving away from the sun look like it is flying backward. Try this experiment to test how the tail of a comet moves.

Cut two pieces of tissue paper 1 inch by 7 inches. This will be the comet's tail. Use

What You Need:

- Blow dryer
- Electrical outlet
- Styrofoam ball
- Drinking straw
- Tissue paper
- Straight pins
- Scissors

your pins to secure the paper to the Styrofoam ball. Push the drinking straw through the bottom of the ball to make the straw a handle.

Hold the comet by the straw and turn on the blow dryer. The blow dryer represents the wind from the sun. Notice how the tail blows away from the sun. Spin your comet around. No matter which way you turn it, the tail blows away from the sun.

To simulate the comet's orbit, have a friend hold the comet and move around you in a circle. Always keep the blow dryer pointing toward the comet. What happens to the comet's tail?

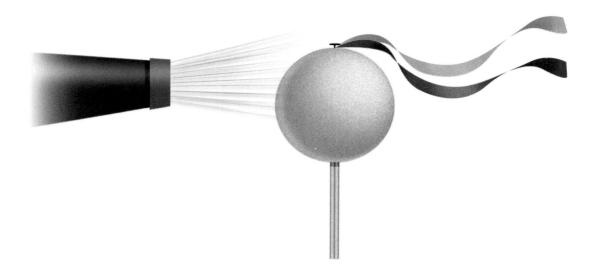

MOON REFLECTIONS

The moon marks off the seasons, and the sun knows when to go down.

Psalm 104:19

Long before King David wrote his psalms, the moon fascinated people. Only 240,000 miles (385,000 kilometers) from the earth, the moon is the earth's closest celestial neighbor and is the brightest object in our night sky. Amazingly, this light we see does not shine from the moon itself. God did not give the moon a light of its own but allows it to glow by reflecting the sun's light.

The moon orbits the earth every 27.3 days and just like the earth, it has a dayside and a night-side. Because of the angle from which we view the moon, it appears to change its shape. Sometimes we see the full reflection of the sun, and the moon appears to be a complete circle. As the moon orbits, we see less of the reflection and the moon appears to be a semicircle, then later a crescent. Because the earth is moving as well as the moon, it takes us over 29 days to see the moon move through all of its phases of reflection. This is called a lunar calendar and was used in biblical times to mark the changing months.

You can chart the phases of the moon to create your own lunar calendar.

Divide your paper into a grid with 30 squares, like a calendar, then number the squares 1 through 30. Each evening after sunset, go outside and observe the moon. Draw a picture to represent what you see. Repeat this every night for 30 days. During that time, you should see the moon progress through all of its phases. Use these illustrations to help you identify the moon phases in your chart.

This project will take a month to complete, but when you are finished you will have a better understanding of God's creation, the moon.

PHASES OF THE MOON

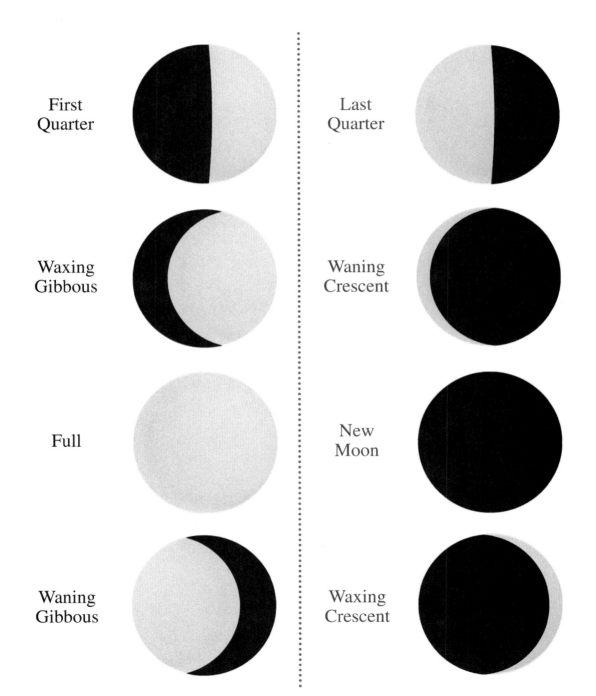

First
Quarter

Last
Quarter

Waxing
Gibbous

Waning
Crescent

Full

New
Moon

Waning
Gibbous

Waxing
Crescent

MOON MOBILE

"It will be established forever like the moon,
the faithful witness in the sky."
Psalm 89:37

Watching the phases of the moon can be fun, but sometimes it is hard to remember the exact order of the changes. Making a moon mobile will help you remember the sequence of moon phases, plus it makes a great room decoration.

Have an adult use the wire cutters to remove the hook from the coat hanger. Shape the wire into a circle. Cut four pieces of string, 20 inches long each. Tie the strings at quarter intervals around the wire circle, and then knot the strings together at the top.

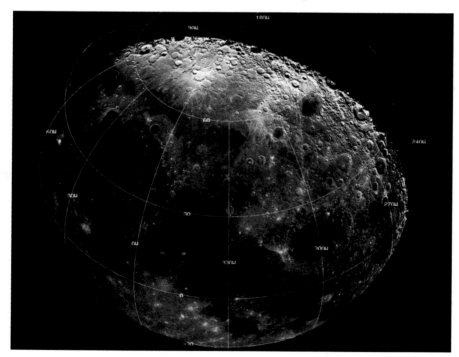

Use the diagrams from "Moon Reflections" (see page 55) for a guide as you cut and illustrate the phases of the moon. Cut eight circles, each 3 inches in diameter. Label each circle with one of the following phases: first quarter, waxing gibbous, full, waning gibbous, last quarter, waning crescent, new moon, waxing crescent. Use the marker to shade in the appropriate section of each "moon."

Cut eight strings, each 12 inches long. Punch a hole in the top of the circles and tie one string to each circle. Then tie the circles to the wire, spacing them evenly. Hang the mobile and watch the moon spin.

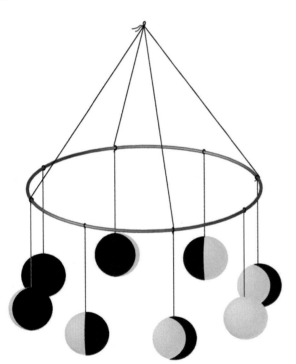

LUNAR ECLIPSE

The sun has one kind of splendor,
the moon another
and the stars another;
and star differs from star in splendor.
I Corinthians 15:41

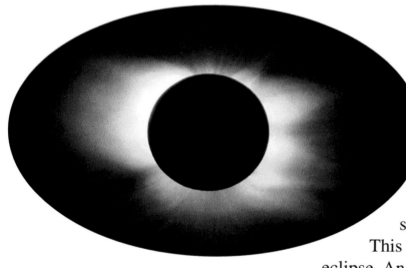

The moon shines in splendor over the earth almost every night, but once in a while the moon's reflection is blocked by the shadow of the earth. This is called a lunar eclipse. An eclipse of the moon can only be seen from the side of the earth that is in darkness.

Eclipses happen on a regular basis, every time the orbits of the earth and moon line up perfectly with the sun. It is interesting to watch a lunar eclipse, and you can find out when the next eclipse will be by consulting an almanac. But if you don't want to wait, you can make your own eclipse right in your living room.

Cover the table with newspapers.

Place one Styrofoam ball on each skewer. The large ball represents the

earth, and the small ball represents the moon. Use the clay to make a stand for each of the skewers. The earth and the moon should be at the same height from the tabletop.

Line the "moon" and "earth" up on the table. Place the light directly behind the earth. The light represents the sun. Slowly move the moon into the shadow of the earth until the earth's shadow blocks the light of the sun (lamp) from reaching the moon. You have just created a lunar eclipse.

What You Need:

- Flat surface
- Old newspapers
- Modeling clay
- Bendable lamp
- Two wooden skewers of equal length
- Styrofoam ball, 3 inches in diameter
- Styrofoam ball, 1 inch in diameter
- Adult supervision

GOD'S GRAVITY

"Dominion and awe belong to God;
he establishes order in the heights of heaven.
Can his forces be numbered?"

Job 25:2-3

Gravity is one of the forces God built into nature. Gravity is the force that attracts objects to each other. It is the reason objects fall to the ground, buildings and people stay on the earth, and it is what causes the earth to orbit the sun.

Every object, from a tiny atom to a giant planet, has a gravitational pull. But gravity is relative to size. The larger the object, the stronger the pull, so living here on Earth we don't feel the gravitational pull of a building or tree because that pull is overcome by the immense pull of the earth's gravity.

While the gravitational pull of an object is relative to its size, the amount of pull each object has is constant. For example, the earth's gravity is the same for a mouse and an elephant. Earth's gravity doesn't pull harder on the elephant because it is bigger.

You can try an experiment to see that God made Earth's gravity constant.

Hold one ball in each hand and stand in front of your partner. Have your partner kneel near the ground to observe which ball hits the ground first. Drop the balls from the exact same height at the exact same time. It is important to keep them exactly the same.

Which ball lands first? If you released the balls at the same time and from the same height, you will learn that they hit the ground at the same time. This will show you that gravity has a constant pull no matter what the weight of an object.

What You Need:

• Two smooth balls of equal size but different weights.

(for example, a hollow plastic ball and a solid rubber ball of the same size)

• A partner to observe and report

ROCKET RACE

The world is firmly established; it cannot be moved.

Psalm 93:1

Gravity is one of God's forces that protects us and keeps us safely on our planet and in our solar system. But gravity is also one of the primary obstacles to space exploration. The earth's gravity not only holds buildings and humans on the earth; it pulls on planes and rockets, too.

It takes an enormous amount of energy to travel out into space and away from the gravity of Earth. This energy is called thrust. Thrust is needed to launch rocket ships and airplanes. It is also used to propel boats, submarines, and small watercrafts. You can experiment with thrust by building your own balloon rocket.

Thread the string through the straw. Have your partner hold one end of the string. Blow up the balloon, but DO NOT tie it shut. Tape the inflated balloon to the straw with the mouth of the balloon facing toward you. Hold your end of the string taut (so that it makes a straight line) and let go of the balloon. The air rushing out of the balloon will rocket it across the string to your partner.

You can experiment to see what will make your balloon rocket fly faster. You might try making wings or fins from the paper and taping them to the balloon. Or you can try increasing the amount of air in your balloon to see if increased amount of "fuel" will make your rocket fly faster.

What You Need:

- Piece of string the length of a room
- Drinking straw
- Balloon
- Computer paper
- Scissors
- Tape
- A partner

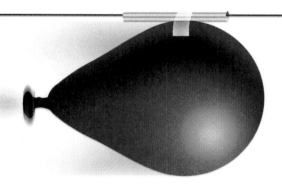

BLAST OFF

He is the Maker of the Bear and Orion,
the Pleiades and the constellations of the south.
He performs wonders that cannot be fathomed,
miracles that cannot be numbered.
Job 9:9-10

Ancient astronomers watched the sky and marveled at the majesty of God's creation. They never imagined that man would one day be able to walk on the moon or view God's creation from a telescope in space.

But through the research of space scientists such as Robert H. Goddard (United States) and Konstantin Tsiolkovsky (Russia), rockets were developed that could reach outer space.

It took much trial and error and the experiments of hundreds of scientists around the world, but on July 16, 1969, the first human walked on the moon. Astronaut Neil Armstrong was the very first person to stand on the moon and look back to marvel at God's creation, the earth.

Today, rockets launch unmanned robots to explore the solar system and space and send information back to humans on earth. The pictures and data they send back show a creation so vast it boggles the imagination. Space is full of stars living, dying, and being born. It has giant gas clouds and spiral galaxies, quasars and voids. The more scientists learn about how huge and magnificent God's creation is, the more we can appreciate how He loves each one of us.

Rockets are an integral part of space exploration. You can create your own rocket with this experiment.

Rinse out a pop bottle and fill it halfway with water. This is now your water rocket. Take the cork and line it up next to the pump needle. Cut the length of the cork so that when the pump needle is inserted into the cork, the end of the needle will stick out of the cork and will be clear to pump air into the bottle.

Place the cork in the bottle. Take the bottle rocket, pump, and the stakes outside. Place the stakes together in a circle the same diameter as the pop bottle. You may have to experiment with the stakes. They should be close enough to support the pop bottle and yet not so tight that they impede the launch.

Place the pump needle inside the cork and make sure the needle is securely attached to the pump. Place the bottle cork-end down inside the stakes, and then start pumping. The air will push out the water and the rocket will soar into the sky. With enough pressure, the rocket can fly up to 100 feet in the air.

What You Need:
- 2-liter empty pop bottle
- Bicycle pump with needle
(the type of needle used to fill up balls with air)
- Cork
- Water
- Six stakes at least two feet tall
(can be metal or wood)
- Open area
(no windows, power lines, or other people)
- Adult supervision

DESIGNED FOR DISTANCE

Praise the LORD from the heavens,
praise him in the heights above.
Praise him, all his angels,
praise him, all his heavenly hosts.
Praise him, sun and moon,
praise him, all you shining stars.
Praise him, you highest heavens
and you waters above the skies.
Let them praise the name of the LORD,
for he commanded and they were created.
Psalm 148:1-5

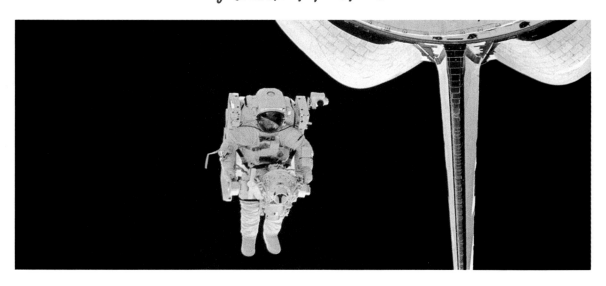

When King David was writing the psalms he could never have imagined that humans would one day have the privilege of learning about God's heavens from firsthand exploration.

The inventions of the rocket and the space shuttle have allowed scientists to gather detailed information about the universe that God created. But gathering this information is extremely difficult. One problem is that space is big. Venus is Earth's closest planetary neighbor, and it is about 25 million miles away. Mars is over 48 million miles from Earth, and the sun is 93 million miles away.

In order to explore space, scientists have had to design ships that move quickly over great distances. There are many factors that can affect the success of a spaceship design. One of those factors is the material used to make a spaceship. The spaceship must be lightweight to reduce the amount of thrust needed to lift off from the earth, but it must also be durable enough to withstand the harsh conditions of space flight.

You can experiment with spaceship design by building a simple rocket made from three different materials.

Trace your rocket pattern onto each of the sheets of material in your supply list. Carefully cut out the pattern. Roll the rectangular shape into a cylinder around the end of the drinking straw. Tape the edge lengthwise. Use the circle shape to form a small cone for the nose of each rocket. Tape the nose to the tip of the rocket.

What You Need:

- Sheet of computer paper
- Sheet of aluminum foil
- Sheet of wax paper
- Rocket pattern (see page 67)
- Sheet of tracing paper
- Scissors
- Pen or pencil
- Drinking straw
- Tape measure

To test the distance each rocket will fly, you will need to mark your launch site. (Your launch site is the place where your feet will be for launch time.) You must stand in the same spot for each rocket launch.

Place the computer paper rocket on the end of your straw and blow. Use the tape measure to see how far your rocket flew. Record the distance and repeat this process with each of the other types of rockets. Which flew the farthest? Run the test two more times to see if you get the same answer.

Scientists constantly work on experiments that will help them learn more about God's universe.

ROCKET PATTERN

2 inches

4 inches

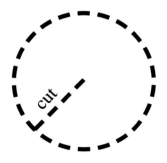

cut

Diameter: 1 ½ inches

SPACE SPLASH

If I go up to the heavens,
you are there...
If I rise on the wings of the dawn,
if I settle on the far side of the sea,
even there your hand will guide me,
your right hand will hold me fast.
Psalm 139:8-10

Leaving the earth's gravitational field is only one problem in space travel. Returning to Earth can be almost as dangerous.

The atmosphere that God placed around our planet protects the earth from falling space rocks by burning them through atmospheric friction. Friction is the force created by one object rubbing against another. You can feel the effect of friction by rubbing your hands together for 15 seconds. The same friction that protects our planet can also burn spaceships.

The first spacecrafts (or space capsules) from the Mercury, Gemini, and Apollo programs could not be reused. They were designed

What You Need:

- *Adult supervision*
- *Step ladder*
- *Raw egg*
- *A variety of "junk"*
  (for example: cloth, string, foam,
  cotton, cardboard boxes,
  egg cartons, and so on)
- *Your imagination*

to be as lightweight and friction free as possible to avoid burning upon reentry into Earth's atmosphere.

Because the space capsules had no landing gear and no real ability to steer in Earth's atmosphere, a parachute was used to slow the capsule's reentry, and the astronauts splashed down into the ocean.

The current space shuttle is launched by a rocket and reenters the earth's atmosphere like a giant glider, coasting to a stop on a specially built runway. The space shuttle can be reused. Landing the first astronauts safely took some incredible planning by researchers. You can try your hand at designing a safe landing craft for your very own "eggstronaut."

Use a raw egg as your passenger and see if you can land it safely from a 10-foot drop.

Create a "spacecraft" that you feel will safely land your egg on the ground. Once you have completed your spacecraft, place your "eggstronaut" inside and get your adult helper. Have the adult climb the ladder to a point where the egg can be dropped 10 feet.

After your spacecraft has landed, check to see if your "eggstronaut" survived reentry.

MISSION TO MARS

...neither height nor depth,
nor anything else in all creation,
will be able to separate us from the love of God
that is in Christ Jesus our Lord.

Romans 8:39

As Paul has told us through the Bible, nothing can separate us from the love of God—not even space travel.

Travel in space is the dream of many people, but the cost of research and materials is very high. Still, some researchers think that there will one day be a space station on the planet Mars. Mars is a logical choice because it is the planet closest to the earth with temperatures that are tolerable.

A Mars space station would need an artificial atmosphere since the Martian atmosphere does not have enough oxygen to keep humans alive. People would have to be housed in some type of protective environment to keep in oxygen and heat.

You can create a simulated space station by building a space dome in your house. (Do not leave this project unsupervised if there are small children in your house.)

Measure and cut the drop cloths into 6-foot by 6-foot squares. Lay them out on the floor according to the diagram (see page 72).

Tape the edges of the plastic together until you have formed a plastic "box" without a lid (see diagram on page 73). Pick one side of the box to be the door. Cut a long slit for the door. Use an extra piece of plastic at least 3 feet wide and as long as the door slit to act as a door flap. Tape this piece of plastic above the door on the inside. Tape only the top.

Take another piece of excess plastic and cut a strip 3 feet wide and 6 feet long. Tape the edges of this together for a short tube. Cut a hole, 2 feet in diameter, in the wall opposite the door.

Tape one edge of the short plastic tube to the outside of the hole. You are forming an air tube to direct wind into your "Mars Colony Space Station." Tape the other end of the tube around the box fan. Remember to make it airtight. If you were really on Mars, this would be your oxygen source.

With the help of an adult, tape one edge of the sixth piece of plastic to one edge of your box. It should look like a box with a hinge. Turn on the box fan as an air source and tape the top of the space station to the other three sides. The box fan should inflate your space station. If it seems to be losing air, check for leaks and repair with tape. Make sure you close the door flap as you enter or leave the space station. This door flap simulates an air lock that would be necessary to keep oxygen inside a real Martian colony's space station.

Once your "Space Station" has been built, you can imagine what it would be like to live on an alien planet. Imagine how exciting it would be to spread God's Word throughout the galaxy!

What You Need:

- Adult supervision
- Seven clear plastic painter's drop cloths (at least 6 feet by 6 feet)
- Three rolls of packing tape
- Box fan
- Scissors
- Tape measure
- Two or three assistants

SPACE STATION DIAGRAM

6 feet

6 feet

6 feet

6 feet

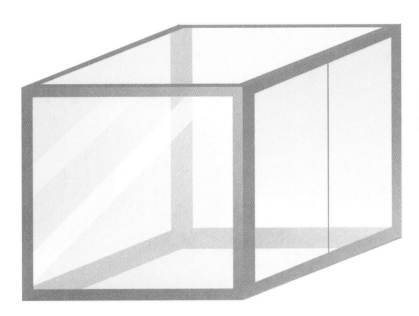

Space Station
Exterior

Space Station
Interior

GOD MADE IT ALL

Praise the LORD.
Praise God in his sanctuary;
praise him in his mighty heavens.
Praise him for his acts of power;
praise him for his surpassing greatness.
Psalm 150:1-2

Stars, moons, planets, and galaxies; God made them all. Scientists, researchers, and astronomers have been working for hundreds of years to learn more about God's creation and how it works. But even with hundreds of people exploring through telescopes, space stations, and rocket trips, humans have learned only a little bit about the universe.

The research goes on constantly. New information and discoveries are made every day and the more humans learn, the more we realize how complex and amazing God's creation really is.

One way to keep up with all the current research is through the Internet. Scientists at NASA and the Jet Propulsion Laboratories keep their Internet web sites current with up-to-the-minute news. You can even view pictures of deep space taken by the Hubble telescope.

You can utilize the Internet as a tool to help you learn more about God's ever changing universe.

If you do not have the Internet in your home, you may be able to use the Internet at your local library or public school.

What You Need:
• Access to the Internet
• Adult Supervision

CHECK OUT THESE WEB SITES

NASA Headquarters ....www.hq.nasa.gov/
NASA Jet Propulsion Laboratory...........www.jpl.nasa.gov/
StarDate Online ....http://stardate.utexas.edu/
SpaceKids...http://spacekids.hq.nasa.gov/
The Astronaut Connection.....................http://nauts.com/
Challenger Center Online......................www.challenger.org/
U.S. Space Camp..................................www.spacecamp.com/main.htm
Thespaceport.com.................................www.space-port.com/
Introduction to Windows
    to the Universe ....www.windows.umich.edu/
NASA Human Spaceflight ....http://spaceflight.nasa.gov/

BIBLIOGRAPHY

Bonnet, Bob and Keen, Dan. *Flight, Space and Astronomy.* New York: Sterling Publishing Company, 1998.

Campbell, Ann-Jeanette. *Amazing Space.* New York: Stonesong Press, 1997.

Couper, Heather and Henbest, Nigel. *How the Universe Works.* London: Reader's Digest Book, 1994.

The Visual Dictionary of the Universe, Eyewitness Visual Dictionaries. New York: Dorling Kindersley, 1993.

Miles, Lisa and Smith, Alastair. *The Usborne Complete Book of Astronomy and Space.* London: Usborne Publishing, 1998.

Stott, Carole. *Space Exploration.* New York: Alfred A. Knopf, 1997.

VanCleave, Janice. *Astronomy for Every Kid.* New York: John Wiley and Sons, 1991.

Weiner, Wendy. *Space.* Westminster: Teacher Created Materials, 1994.

Meet Stephanie Finke: I am an educator with over seventeen years of experience. Over those years, I have been privileged to teach in a variety of settings including public, private, and parochial schools. I also served as the director of children's education at Missouri Botanical Garden.

My experience with children has led me to realize that many people, even Christians, tend to view science as separate and apart from God. Growing up with a biology teacher as a father, I was always taught that science is just a tool we use to learn more about God's creation. Without God, there would be no science.

Currently, I am a second grade teacher at Benton Elementary School in St. Charles, Missouri where I try to instill a sense of wonder and a quest for knowledge in my students. At home, I use my two children, Nichole and Joshua, as guinea pigs for my experiments. They have become experts at exploding rockets and cleaning up lava spills. My husband Alan has learned to ignore the strange things that grow in our refrigerator and nobody has eaten one of my experiments. . .yet!